Piggyback Songs To Sign

Written by Jean Warren and Susan Shroyer

Illustrated by Joan Kimmel
Chorded by Barbara Robinson

Totline® Publications
A Division of Frank Schaffer Publications, Inc.
Torrance, California

Editorial Staff:
> Gayle Bittinger, Kathleen Cubley, Brenda Mann Harrison,
> Erica West, Brenda Lalonde

Production Staff:
> Jo Anna Brock, Jill Lustig, Sarah Ness, Eric Stovall

Piggyback® is a registered trademark of Totline® Publications.

ISBN 0-911019-53-7

Library of Congress Catalog Card Number 85-50433
Printed in the United States of America
Published by: Totline® Publications.

Business Office: 23740 Hawthorne Blvd.
                    Torrance, CA 90505

Contents

Introduction

Writing the songs in *Piggyback Songs to Sign* has been an enjoyable experience for me, and I hope that teaching children to sign in this simple way will be an enjoyable experience for both you and your children.

I wish to thank Susan Shroyer for writing the sign language descriptions in the book.

Jean Warren

The term *sign language* is a generic term that indicates any form of manual communication. There are many different sign language systems, but American Sign Language (ASL) is the native language of most deaf Americans. It is a visual, gestural language with its own grammatical rules and it is not English. Various systems of signing have been developed over the years that use much of the vocabulary of ASL, but in the context of English. These systems are often easier for native English speakers to learn because they follow English word order and the rules of English grammar.

The signs in *Piggyback Songs to Sign* are a combination of ASL and English signs. If a word has more than one sign, the sign shown is one that is easier for 3- to 5-year-olds to learn. Some signs were adapted for simplicity.

Many phrases are signed in English with signs for each English word and grammatical markings, such as verb tenses. These words can be signed for a more English approach to signing, but may also be eliminated to make the phrase easier for a young child to sign.

ASL does not incorporate English words, such as *the*, *a* or the verb *to be*, because these words offer little or no real meaning to what is being signed. For example, the ASL sign for the word *snow* can be used alone to convey the meaning of the English phrase *it is snowing* or the entire phrase may be used. This is left to the discretion of the teacher.

Some phrases in the book are signed as they would be in ASL because of simplicity and because ASL better indicates the meaning of the phrase. The manual alphabet is included in the book for clarification of handshapes used in the phrase descriptions and for fingerspelling use with your children.

Signing to song is a fun and easy way to learn to sign and an excellent way to teach young children to recognize and accept differences in others. Have fun!

Susan Shroyer

What Is Your Name?

What

Index finger of right hand moves over extended fingers of left hand. Each finger of the left hand represents an option.

Is

Right pinkie (*i* handshape) starts on lower lip and moves straight out.

Your

Opened right hand moves toward person to whom you are speaking.

Name

Place index and middle fingers of right hand on index and middle fingers of left hand, with palms facing each other at a 90° angle.

I Like You

Sung to: *Skip to My Lou*

C
I like you, yes, I do,
G₇
I like you, yes, I do,
C
I like you, yes, I do.
G₇   C
What is your name?

Jean Warren

I'd Like to Meet You

Sung to: *Skip to My Lou*

C
I'd like to meet you,

What is your name?
G₇
I'd like to meet you,

What is your name?
C
I'd like to meet you,

What is your name?
G₇   C
I like making friends.

Jean Warren

What Is Your Name?

Sung to: *Hush, Little Baby*

C   G₇
What is your name? I'd like to know.
                         C
What is your name? I'd like to know.
                           G₇
Please won't you tell me before I go?
                         C
What is your name? I'd like to know.

Jean Warren

I'd Like to Know You Better

Sung to: *Little White Duck*

C₇   F
What is your name?
            C₇
Is it Bob or Mary?

What is your name?
            F
Is it Sue or Larry?
 B♭
I spent all day
            F
Wondering what to say,
     G₇
In case you happened
     C₇
To come my way,
         F
Oh, **what is your name?**
              C₇
I'd like to know you better.
C   C₇   F
What is your name?

Jean Warren

Hello, New Friend

Hello

Wave right hand with fingers together and palm out.

New

Turn both palms up. Right palm crosses over left palm, moving forward and up.

Friend

Interlock right and left index fingers, with right index finger over left.

New Face
Sung to: *Frere Jacques*

C
When I see

A new face

You'll hear me

Say hello.

Hello, new friend,

Hello, new friend,

When I see

A new face.

Jean Warren

New Friends
Sung to: *Oh, What a Beautiful Morning*

C   Bb   F
Hello, new friend, how are you?
C   G7
Hello, new friend of mine.
C   F   F#dim
I am so glad I met you,
C   G7   C
New friends are hard to find!

Jean Warren

Hello, New Friend
Sung to: *Frere Jacques*

C
Hello, new friend, hello, new friend,

What is your name? What is your name?

I am so glad that I have

Met you, my new friend.

Hello, new friend, hello, new friend.

Jean Warren

Stay and Play
Sung to: *The Bear Went Over the Mountain*

C   F   C
Hello, new friend, I like you,
G7   C
Hello, new friend, I like you,
                                    F
Hello, new friend, I like you,
G7   C
Do you want to play?

C   F   C
Hello, new friend, I like you,
G7   C
Hello, new friend, I like you,
                                    F
Hello, new friend, I like you,
 G7   C
I hope that you can stay.

Jean Warren

At Our School Today

At

Fingertips of right hand touch back of left hand.

Our

Place cupped right hand on right side of chest, with thumb touching chest. Move hand in arc to left side of chest, ending with pinkie touching chest.

School

Clap right hand, with palm down and fingers pointing left, twice on left hand, with palm up and fingers pointing right.

Today

Cupped hands, with palms up, move in a slight downward motion.

This Is the Way

Sung to: *The Mulberry Bush*

D
This is the way we play with blocks,
A₇
Play with blocks, play with blocks.
D
This is the way we play with blocks,
A₇   D
At our school today.

Additional verses: This is the way we play outside; We play with clay; We read our books; We cut and paste; We climb and swing.

Jean Warren

At Our School Today

Sung to: *London Bridge*

C
At our school today we played,
G₇   C
Today we played, today we played.

At our school today we played,
G₇   C
It was lots of fun.
C
At our school today we read,
G₇   C
Today we read, today we read,

At our school today we read,
G₇   C
It was lots of fun.

Additional verses: At our school today we painted; cooked; danced.

Jean Warren

Working Together

Sung to: *Here We Go Looby Lou*

D
Let's all make a boat,
                          A₇
Let's all make a boat,
D
Let's all make a boat,
A₇   D
At our school today.

Additional verses: Let's all make some bread; write a story; sing a song.

Jean Warren

School Time

Sung to: *Found a Peanut*

D
At our school, at our school,
                        A₇
At our school today,
                  D
We worked so hard, so very hard,
          A₇   D
Then we went outside to play.

Jean Warren

Harvest Time

Harvest

Bent index finger of right hand sweeps over fisted left hand as if cutting stalks of wheat.

Time

Bent index finger of right hand taps wrist of left hand, where a watch is generally worn.

Dig, Dig
Sung to: *Row, Row, Row Your Boat*

C
Dig, dig, it's **harvest time,**

Dig down in the ground.

Pull out all the vegetables
G₇   C
Big and ripe and round.

C
Pick, pick, it's **harvest time,**

Pick high in the tree,

Gather all the harvest fruit,
   G₇   C
That you and I can see.

Jean Warren

Time to Pick the Crops
Sung to: *Jingle Bells*

C
Harvest time, harvest time,

Time to pick the crops.
F   C
Harvest time, harvest time,
G₇
When the growing stops.
C
Dig them up, pick them off,

Gather them just right.
F   C
They'll taste good when winter's here,
     G₇   C
When the ground is covered white.

Jean Warren

Pick the Apples
Sung to: *The Paw Paw Patch*

F
Let's pick the apples, it's **harvest time,**
C₇
Let's pick the apples, it's **harvest time,**
F
Let's pick the apples, it's **harvest time,**
C₇   F
Way down yonder in the apple orchards.

Jean Warren

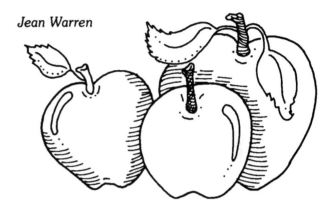

Hurray, It's Harvest Time
Sung to: *Shoo Fly*

F   C
Hurray, it's **harvest time,**
                     F
Hurray, it's **harvest time,**
                     C
Hurray, it's **harvest time,**
                     F
Now we can pick the fruit.

F   C
Hurray, it's **harvest time,**
                     F
Hurray, it's **harvest time,**
                     C
Hurray, it's **harvest time,**
                     F
Now we can dig the vegetables.

Jean Warren

Leaves Are Falling

Leaves Are Falling

Place wrist of right hand on left index finger. Let right hand hang limp like a leaf and shake it from side to side. Then drop right hand while shaking it, indicating a falling leaf.

All Over Town
Sung to: *The Bear Went Over the Mountain*

    C   F   C
The **leaves are falling** this autumn,
    G_7 C
The **leaves are falling** this autumn,
                          F
The **leaves are falling** this autumn,
G_7 C
Falling all over town.

Jean Warren

Leaves Are Falling on My Nose
Sung to: *Jingle Bells*

C
Leaves are falling,

Leaves are falling,

One fell on my nose.
F
Leaves are falling,
C
Leaves are falling,
G_7
One fell on my toes.
C
Leaves are falling,

Leaves are falling,

One fell on my head.
F
Leaves are falling,
C
Leaves are falling,
G_7
Yellow, orange and red.

Jean Warren

Give a Little Cheer
Sung to: *Yankee Doodle*

           F C_7
When **leaves are falling** on the ground,
F C_7
I give a little cheer.
           F B^b
When **leaves are falling** on the ground,
   C   F
It means that winter's near.
B^b
Leaves are falling, yes, siree,
F
Falling on the ground.
B^b
Leaves are falling, can't you see?
F C_7 F
Red and orange and brown.

Jean Warren

Red, Yellow, Brown
Sung to: *Frere Jacques*

C
Leaves are falling,

Leaves are falling,

All around,

In the town.

Leaves are falling,

Leaves are falling,

Red, yellow, brown,

Red, yellow, brown.

Jean Warren

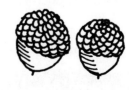

Here's a Little Pumpkin

Here's

Both hands, with palms up, move out in opposite circles. Fisted right hand (s handshape) flips to left to show the contraction.

a

Closed right hand with thumb to the side (a handshape) moves to right.

Little

Index fingers of both hands, with palms facing each other and thumbs up (l handshapes), point away from body. Move palms slightly toward each other.

Pumpkin

Middle finger of right hand, with index finger extended out and middle finger down (p handshape), taps back of fisted left hand as if thumping a melon.

Growing on the Vine

Sung to: *The Farmer in the Dell*

Oh, **here's a little pumpkin,**
D

Oh, **here's a little pumpkin.**

Heigh-ho, the derry-oh,

It's growing oh, so fine.
A₇   D

Oh, **here's a little pumpkin,**
D

Oh, **here's a little pumpkin.**

Heigh-ho, the derry-oh,

We'll pick it off the vine.
A₇   D

Jean Warren

Little Pumpkin

Sung to: *The Mulberry Bush*

Here's a little pumpkin,
D

Pumpkin, pumpkin.
A₇

Here's a little pumpkin,
D

With a great big grin.
A₇   D

Jean Warren

Here's a Little Pumpkin

Sung to: *Go In and Out the Window*

Oh, **here's a little pumpkin,**
F   C

Oh, **here's a little pumpkin,**
F

Oh, **here's a little pumpkin,**
C

Small and orange and round.
F

Oh, **here's a little pumpkin,**
F   C

Oh, **here's a little pumpkin,**
F

Oh, **here's a little pumpkin,**
C

The best that I have found.
F

Jean Warren

Orange and Round

Sung to: *I'm a Little Teapot*

Here's a little pumpkin,
C

Orange and round,
F   C

Here's a little pumpkin,
G₇   C

That I found.
G₇   C

When I get him cleaned up

I will say,
F   C

"Here's a little pumpkin

For my holiday."

Jean Warren

Happy Halloween

Happy

Tap chest with right palm, moving palm up and forward twice.

Halloween

Turn palms of both hands toward self and touch eyes with first two fingers of both hands (*h* handshapes). Turn palms away from self and touch temples with index fingers.

See the Goblins

Sung to: *The Farmer in the Dell*

Oh, **Happy Halloween,**
D

Oh, **Happy Halloween,**

See the goblins? What a sight!

Oh, **Happy Halloween.**
A₇   D

Additional verses: Have some fun this
scary night; Jack - o'- lanterns glow so bright.

Jean Warren

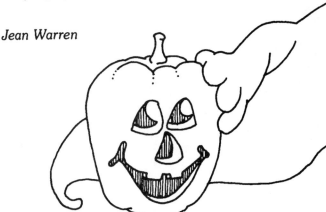

Halloween Greetings

Sung to: *Someone's in the Kitchen
  With Dinah*

Happy Halloween to Lisa.
C

Happy Halloween to Andrew.
G₇

Happy Halloween to Kathleen.
C

Happy Halloween to Sue.
G₇   C

Substitute the names of your children for
the names in the song.

Jean Warren

October 31st

Sung to: *For He's a Jolly Good Fellow*

Oh, **Happy Halloween,**
C   F C

Oh, **Happy Halloween,**
G₇   C

Oh, **Happy Halloween,**
F

It's October 31st.
C   G₇ C

Jean Warren

A Safe Halloween

Sung to: *The Farmer in the Dell*

Happy Halloween,
D

A safe Halloween.

It is Halloween tonight,

What a scary sight.
A₇   D

Happy Halloween,
D

A safe Halloween.

It is Halloween tonight,

Carry a big light.
A₇   D

Jean Warren

Trick or Treat

Trick or Treat

Place thumbs between first two fingers (*t* handshapes) on both hands. Move hands once in a backward bike-pedaling motion.

Big Red Nose
Sung to: *Frere Jacques*

C
Trick or treat, trick or treat,

Big red nose, great big feet.

I'm a jolly clown,

I bend up and down.

Trick or treat, trick or treat.

Jean Warren

We're All Dressed Up
Sung to: *She'll Be Coming Round the Mountain*

      C
Oh, we're all dressed up in costumes,

Trick or treat.

Oh, we're all dressed up in costumes,
     G₇
Trick or treat.
    C
Oh, we're all dressed up in costumes,
    F
Yes, we're all dressed up in costumes.
    C   G₇
Oh, we're all dressed up in costumes,
    C
Trick or treat.

Jean Warren

Halloween Night
Sung to: *Three Blind Mice*

C   G₇   C   G₇   C
Trick or treat, trick or treat.
    G₇   C   G₇   C
It's so neat, it's so neat.
       G₇   C
I like to dress up on Halloween night,
      G₇   C
In my costume, I make a grand sight,
      G₇   C
I walk around with a great big flashlight,
      G₇   C
Trick or treat!

Jean Warren

It's So Neat
Sung to: *Frere Jacques*

C
Trick or treat, trick or treat,

It's so neat, it's so neat.

I see big black cats,

I see small black bats.

Trick or treat, it's so neat.

Jean Warren

Happy Thanksgiving

Happy

Tap chest with right palm, moving palm up and forward twice.

Thanksgiving

Fingertips of both hands touch lips. Hands move out and down and then forward as if presenting something.

Oh, What a Happy Day
Sung to: *Oh, What a Beautiful Morning*

C   Bᵇ   F
Oh, what a **Happy Thanksgiving,**
C   G₇
Oh, what a happy day.
C   F   F#dim
We'll eat some pie and some turkey,
C   G₇   C
Happy Thanksgiving today.

C   Bᵇ   F
Oh, what a **Happy Thanksgiving,**
C   G₇
Oh, what a happy day.
C   F   F#dim
We'll see our friends and our family,
C   G₇   C
Happy Thanksgiving today.

Jean Warren

A Special Day
Sung to: *Skip to My Lou*

F
Happy Thanksgiving,

We're on our way.
C₇
Happy Thanksgiving,

A special day.
F
Happy Thanksgiving,

We'll eat and play,
C₇   F
When we get to Grandma's.

Jean Warren

Let's Celebrate
Sung to: *Frere Jacques*

C
Happy Thanksgiving,

Happy Thanksgiving,

I can't wait, let's celebrate.

I will bring the turkey,

You can bring the pies.

Happy Thanksgiving,

Happy Thanksgiving.

Jean Warren

Happy Thanksgiving
Sung to: *Happy Birthday*

               F   C
Happy Thanksgiving to you,
                     F
Happy Thanksgiving to you.

Happy Thanksgiving,
               Bᵇ
Happy Thanksgiving,
           F   C   F
Happy Thanksgiving to you.

Gayle Bittinger

We Give Thanks

We

Place pinkie and thumb of right hand together (*w* handshape) and touch index finger to right shoulder. Swing handshape to left until ring finger touches left shoulder.

Give

Hands, with palms up, move forward as if presenting something.

Thanks

Fingertips of right hand touch lips. Right hand moves out and down. Add *s* handshape for correct English grammar.

Let's Have a Celebration
Sung to: *Oh, My Darling Clementine*

C
We give thanks, we give thanks

              G
For our family, friends and nation.

                 C
We give thanks, we give thanks,

G   C
Let us have a celebration.

Jean Warren

Treasures of Our Land
Sung to: *This Old Man*

C
We give thanks,

We give thanks

F   G
For the treasures of this land,

        C
From the mountains high

Filled with giant trees,

G   C G C
Down the rivers to the seas.

C
We give thanks,

We give thanks

F   G
For the treasures of this land,

        C
From the great farm lands

To the lone prairie,

G   C G C
It's the land for you and me.

Jean Warren

For Family and Friends
Sung to: *Three Blind Mice*

C G$_7$ C   G$_7$ C
We give thanks, we give thanks

    G$_7$ C   G$_7$ C
For our family, for our friends.

        G$_7$ C
We wish that we could always be

         G$_7$ C
With special friends and family,

               G$_7$ C
'Cause they're the sights we love to see.

    G$_7$ C
We give thanks.

Jean Warren

We Give Thanks
Sung to: *When Johnny Comes Marching Home*

      Em
When the table's set with food to eat,

G
We give thanks.

      Em
When nighttime comes and we are safe,

G   B$_7$
We give thanks.

   G   D$_7$
We bow our heads and fold our hands

     Em   B$_7$
And pray for peace across our lands,

       Em Am Em B$_7$
For we all want peace,

      Em
For this **we give thanks.**

Jean Warren

Great Big Turkey

Great Big

Bent fingers of both hands touch, with palms facing each other. Pull hands apart, indicating a large amount of something.

Turkey

Place right hand, with index finger and thumb extended down (q handshape), on chin. Wiggle hand slightly front to back, indicating the turkey's wattle.

Wobble, Wobble

Sung to: *London Bridge*

C
Great big turkey dance and sing,
G   C
Dance and sing, dance and sing.

Great big turkey dance and sing
G   C
While you flap your wings.

C
Great big turkey dance and gobble,
G   C
Dance and gobble, dance and gobble.

Great big turkey dance and gobble
G   C
While you wobble, wobble.

Jean Warren

Hear Him Gobble

Sung to: *Frere Jacques*

C
Great big turkey,

Great big turkey.

Hear him gobble,

Watch him wobble.

Running all around,

Making such a sound.

Great big turkey,

Great big turkey.

Jean Warren

Great Big Turkey

Sung to: *She'll Be Coming Round the Mountain*

              F
We'll cook up a **great big turkey,** Thanksgiving,
                                            C₇
We'll cook up a **great big turkey,** Thanksgiving.
              F
We'll cook up a **great big turkey,**
              B♭
We'll cook up a **great big turkey,**
              F   C₇   F
We'll cook up a **great big turkey,** Thanksgiving.

Jean Warren

I'm a Great Big Turkey

Sung to: *I'm a Little Teapot*

C
I'm a **great big turkey,**
F   C
Listen to my sound.
G₇   C
I just love to gobble
        G₇   C
As I strut around.

When I get all puffed up,
F   C
I gobble night and day.
              F
I'm a **great big turkey**
        G₇   C
And this is what I say,

"Gobble, gobble, gobble."

Jean Warren

Indians and Pilgrims

Indians

Index finger and thumb of right hand form a circle, leaving other fingers extended (*f* handshape). Pull hand from corner of mouth toward ear to indicate warpaint. Add *s* handshape for correct English grammar.

and

Right hand makes *5* handshape, then moves to right and closes to *o* handshape.

Pilgrims

Place index fingers of both hands on chest and draw outline of a Pilgrim's collar. Add *s* handshape for correct English grammar.

Autumn Feast

Sung to: *The Battle Hymn of the Republic*

The ^{B♭} **Indians and Pilgrims**

Had a feast one autumn day.

They ^{E♭} sat down at a table

Where ^{B♭} a great big turkey lay.

They passed the corn and passed the bread

And ^{Cm} passed the ^{B♭} pumpkin ^F pie. ^{B♭}

Then ^{B♭} the **Indians and Pilgrims**

Said, ^{Cm} "Let's ^{B♭} give ^F peace a ^{B♭} try."

Jean Warren

Live in Peace

Sung to: *When Johnny Comes Marching Home*

Oh, the ^{Em} **Indians and Pilgrims** went

Hand-^Gin-hand,

Oh, the ^{Em} **Indians and Pilgrims** went

Hand-^Gin-hand. ^{B₇}

They ^G saw the deer, they ^{D₇} saw the corn,

They ^{Em} saw a nation as ^{B₇} it was born,

And ^{Em Am Em} they were all so glad

They ^{B₇} learned ^{Em} to live in ^{Am} peace. ^{Em}

Jean Warren

Indians and Pilgrims

Sung to: *Jingle Bells*

The ^F **Indians and Pilgrims**

Had a great big feast,

And ^{C₇} when it was over ^F

They ^{G₇} smoked a pipe of ^{C₇} peace.

The ^F **Indians and Pilgrims**

Learned to share this land,

And ^{C₇} every Thanksgiving ^F

We ^{C₇} give them a big ^F hand. (Clap.)

Jean Warren

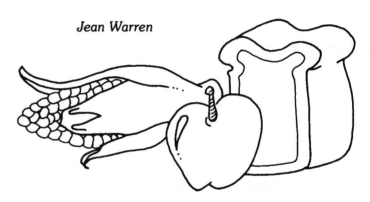

We Will Have a Party

Sung to: *When the Saints Come Marching In*

Oh, when the ^C **Indians and Pilgrims** come,

Oh, when the **Indians and Pilgrims** ^G come,

We ^C will have a ^F great big party,

When ^C the **Indians** ^{G₇} and **Pilgrims** ^C come.

Jean Warren

Happy Holidays

Happy

Tap chest with right palm, moving palm up and forward twice.

Holidays

Hold first two fingers of both hands out and together (*h* handshapes). Thumbs tap chest. Add *s* handshape for correct English grammar.

Season of Good Cheer
Sung to: *Jingle Bells*

F
Happy days, happy days,

Happy holidays.
C₇   F
'Tis the season of good cheer
G₇   C
In so many ways.

F
Happy days, happy days,

Happy holidays.
C₇   F
Everyone's so happy
C₇   F
Happy holidays!

Jean Warren

I Can't Wait
Sung to: *Frere Jacques*

C
Happy holidays,

Happy holidays.

Presents to make,

Goodies to bake.

I can't wait to start,

I can't wait to start.

Happy holidays,

Happy holidays.

Jean Warren

It's Time
Sung to: *The Farmer in the Dell*

       D
It's time to decorate,

It's time celebrate,

Heigh-ho, the derry-oh,
      A₇   D
Happy holidays.

       D
It's time to dance and sing,

It's time for gifts to bring,

Heigh-ho, the derry-oh,
      A₇   D
Happy holidays.

Jean Warren

Happy Holidays
Sung to: *Camptown Races*

C
All join hands and sing this song,
G₇
Happy holidays.
C
Santa's coming won't be long,
G₇   C
Happy holidays.
              F   C
Happy holidays, happy holidays.

We'll circle round then all sit down,
G₇   C
Happy holidays.

Jean Warren

Spin the Dreidel

Spin the Dreidel

Place right index finger, pointed down, over raised left index finger. Circle right index finger quickly around left index finger, indicating a spinning dreidel.

Win or Lose

Sung to: *Oh, My Darling Clementine*

G
Spin the dreidel, spin the dreidel,
D₇
Oh, what will it say?

G
Win or lose, win or lose,
D₇   G
Spin the dreidel and play.

Jean Warren

Round and Round

Sung to: *Twinkle, Twinkle, Little Star*

C   F   C
Spin the dreidel round and round,
G₇   C   G₇   C
Watch it spin and then fall down.
F   C   G₇
Will I lose? Will I win?
C   G₇   C   G₇
Spin the dreidel, spin, spin, spin.
C   F   C
Spin the dreidel round and round,
G₇   C   G₇   C
Watch it spin and then fall down.

Jean Warren

It Is Hanukkah

Sung to: *Mary Had a Little Lamb*

C
Can we please **spin the dreidel,**
G₇   C
Spin the dreidel, spin the dreidel?
C
Can we please **spin the dreidel?**
G₇   C
It is Hanukkah.

Jean Warren

Little Dreidel

Sung to: *Yankee Doodle*

C   G₇
Once I found a little dreidel
C   G₇
Lying on the floor.
           C   F
And when I gave it a big spin
      G₇   C
It spun right out the door.
F
Spin the dreidel round and round,
C
Spin the dreidel slowly.
F
Spin the dreidel carefully
          C   G₇   C
And watch where it might go.

Jean Warren

Light the Candles

Light

Place left hand, with palm facing right, in front of body. Bring right hand up, "striking" left palm with thumbnail as if striking a match.

the

Place thumb between first two fingers of right hand (*t* handshape). Move hand to right.

Candles

Place right *5* handshape, with palm facing out, on index finger of left hand, with palm facing self. Wiggle fingers to indicate the motion of a flame. Add *s* handshape for correct English grammar.

We're Going to Light the Candles

Sung to: *The Bear Went Over the Mountain*

F   B♭   F
We're going to **light the candles,**
C   F
We're going to **light the candles,**
                    B♭
We're going to **light the candles**
F   C F   C F
Because it's (Hannukah/Christmas time).

Jean Warren

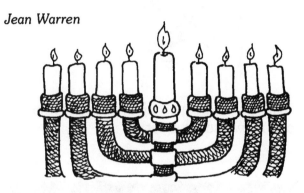

Standing in a Row

Sung to: *The Eensy, Weensy Spider*

C
When I **light the candles,**
 G₇   C
I hold the light just so.

I love to **light the candles,**
     G₇   C
And watch the flames glow.

Pretty (Hannukah/Christmas) candles,
G₇   C
Standing in a row.

I love to watch the candles,
 G₇   C
Until they burn down low.

Jean Warren

Light the Candles

Sung to: *Did You Ever See a Lassie?*

      F
It's time to **light the candles,**
   C   F
The candles, the candles.

It's time to **light the candles**
    C   C   F
On (Hannukah/Christmas) night.
    C   F
The big ones, the little ones,
    C   F
The short ones, the tall ones,

It's time to **light the candles**
    C   C   F
On (Hannukah/Christmas) night.

Jean Warren

One by One

Sung to: *Frere Jacques*

C
Light the candles, light the candles,

One by one, one by one.

It is time for (Hannukah/Christmas),

It is time for (Hannukah/Christmas).

Light the candles, light the candles.

Jean Warren

Santa Claus Is Coming

Santa Claus

Cupped right hand (*c* handshape), with palm facing left, touches chin, then flips and moves down to stomach, indicating Santa's beard.

Is

Right pinkie (*i* handshape) starts on lower lip and moves straight out.

Coming

Index fingers of both hands, with palms facing self, alternately roll toward body. An *i* handshape twists to right to add *-ing* for correct English grammar.

Christmas Eve

Sung to: *It's Raining, It's Pouring*

C
It's Christmas Eve,

And **Santa Claus is coming.**

G₇
I put a stocking out for him,

C
I can't wait until morning.

It's Christmas Eve,

And **Santa Claus is coming.**

G₇
I put some snacks out for him,

C
I hope that he is hungry.

Jean Warren

Hip, Hip Hurray

Sung to: *Did You Ever See a Lassie?*

C
Oh, **Santa Claus is coming,**

G₇   C
In five days, in five days.

Oh, **Santa Claus is coming,**

G₇   C
Hip, hip hurray.

Substitute the number of days left until
Christmas Eve for the word *five.*

Jean Warren

Santa Claus Is Coming

Sung to: *Yankee Doodle*

C   G₇
Santa Claus is coming to town,

C   G₇
He drives a great big sleigh.

C   F
He fills the stockings one by one,

G₇   C
Then hurries on his way.

F
Santa Claus is coming,

C
Santa Claus is near.

F
Santa Claus is coming

C   G₇   C
To bring us Christmas cheer.

Jean Warren

I Wonder What He'll Bring

Sung to: *The Battle Hymn of the Republic*

B♭
Santa Claus is coming,

I can hear his sleigh bells ring.

E♭
Santa Claus is coming,

B♭
I wonder what he'll bring.

I hope he has a great big pack

Filled with lots of toys,

Cm   F   B♭
All for the girls and boys.

Jean Warren

Happy New Year

Happy

Tap chest with right palm, moving palm up and forward twice.

New

Turn both palms up. Right palm crosses over left palm, moving forward and up.

Year

Right fist rests on left fist, then circles around and rests on left fist again, indicating the revolution of the earth around the sun.

It's Almost Time

Sung to: *Little White Duck*

C₇   F
Oh, it's almost time

                C₇
To say, **"Happy New Year."**

It's almost time

               F
To give a great big cheer.

      B♭
We'll blow our horns

      F
And have some fun,

        G₇
And count from three

C₇
Back to one.

         F
Oh, it's almost time

               C₇
To say, **"Happy New Year."**

Three-two-one.

C   C₇   F
"Happy New Year!"

Jean Warren

Hurray!

Sung to: *The Farmer in the Dell*

    D
Oh, **Happy New Year.**

Oh, **Happy New Year.**

Let's toot our horns and celebrate,

            A₇   D
With a great big cheer. Hurray!

Kathleen Cubley

Everybody Give a Cheer

Sung to: *Bingo*

F   B♭   F
Everybody give a cheer,

          C₇   F
For a **Happy New Year.**

     B♭
H-A-P-P-Y,

C₇   F
H-A-P-P-Y,

     B♭
H-A-P-P-Y,

        C₇   F
For a **Happy New Year.**

Jean Warren

Happy New Year

Sung to: *You Are My Sunshine*

              C
Oh, **Happy New Year,**

Oh, **Happy New Year!**

             F
The bells are ringing,

         C
Oh, what fun!

       F
I love to blow horns

                C
And throw confetti.

                   G₇   C
Happy New Year, everyone!

Jean Warren

Hand-in-Hand

Hand-in-Hand

Place both closed hands (*a* handshapes), with heels together. Then move hands out together. This sign also is used for "together."

Wear a Smile

Sung to: *The Battle Hymn of the Republic*

B♭
I always wear a smile

When I'm walking **hand-in-hand,**
E♭
I always wear a smile
　　　B♭
When I'm working **hand-in-hand,**

I always wear a smile

When I'm playing **hand-in-hand,**
　　　Cm　　　B♭　F　B♭
And my smile goes on and on.

Refrain:
B♭
Walking, walking **hand-in-hand,**
E♭　　　　　　　　　　B♭
Working, working **hand-in-hand,**

Playing, playing **hand-in-hand,**
　　　Cm　　　B♭　F　B♭
And my smile goes on and on.

Jean Warren

Hand-in-Hand

Sung to: *The Muffin Man*

G
Dr. King walked **hand-in-hand,**
C　　　　　　　D₇
Hand-in-hand, hand-in-hand.
G
Dr. King walked **hand-in-hand,**
　　　D₇　　G
With everyone.

G
We can walk just like he did,
C　　　　　D₇
Like he did, like he did.
G
We can walk just like he did,
D₇　　　　　G
Hand-in-hand.

Jean Warren

Dr. King Marched

Sung to: *Row, Row, Row Your Boat*

C
Hand-in-hand he marched

Down every lane and street.

He always opened up his heart
　　　G　　　　　　　C
To everyone he'd meet.

C
Hand-in-hand he marched

With brothers one and all.

That is why we say today,
　　　G　　　　　　　C
He always stood so tall.

Jean Warren

It Is Snowing

It

Place left hand, with palm facing right, in front of self. Move tip of right pinkie (*i* handshape) into left palm.

Is

Right pinkie (*i* handshape) starts on lower lip and moves straight out.

Snowing

Extend fingers of both hands with palms facing down. Fingers wiggle and move down like falling snowflakes. An *i* handshape twists to right to add *-ing* for correct English grammar.

All Around

Sung to: *Frere Jacques*

C
It is snowing, it is snowing,

All around, on the ground.

I can hear the silence,

I can hear the silence.

It is snowing, it is snowing.

Jean Warren

It Is Snowing

Sung to: *Oh, Dear What Can the Matter Be?*

C
Oh, dear, **it is snowing,**
G₇
Oh, dear, **it is snowing,**
C
Oh, dear, **it is snowing.**
G₇   C
What is it snowing on?

C
It is snowing on my nose,
G₇
It is snowing on my toes,
C
It is snowing on my clothes.
G₇   C
That's what **it is snowing** on.

Jean Warren

Snowing All Around

Sung to: *Pop! Goes the Weasel*

D   A₇   D
All around the neighborhood,
          A₇   D
See, **it is snowing.**
          A₇   D
That is why the boys and girls
A₇   D
Outside are going.

D   A₇   D
Round and round the yard they go,
          A₇   D
Happy **it is snowing.**
                  A₇   D
Watch them roll a great big ball,
A₇   D
See, it is growing.

Jean Warren

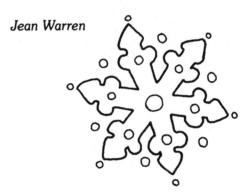

Snow Is Falling

Sung to: *You Are My Sunshine*

                        C
Oh, **it is snowing,** oh, **it is snowing,**
              F   C
The snow is falling all around.
                F   C
I hope it snows long, I hope it snows strong,
              G₇   C
Until it covers up the ground.

Jean Warren

Winter Fun

Winter

Pinkie and thumb of each hand touch with other fingers extended and palms out (*w* handshapes). Move handshapes back and forth as if shivering.

Fun

Index and middle fingers of right hand (*h* handshape) touch nose, then move to index and middle fingers of left hand, with both palms down.

When Snow Starts Falling

Sung to: *When Johnny Comes Marching Home*

      Em
When snow starts falling all around,

      G
There's **winter fun.**

      Em
When snow starts sticking on the ground,

    G   B₇
There's **winter fun.**

    G   D₇
We'll build a snowman big and tall,

    Em   B₇
And slide down hills and slip and fall.

    Em   Am   Em
And when we're done

B₇   Em
We'll still have **winter fun.**

Jean Warren

Winter Fun at Last

Sung to: *The Farmer in the Dell*

         D
The snow is falling slow,

The snow is falling fast.

Heigh-ho, just watch it snow,

A₇   D
Winter fun at last!

Jean Warren

Falling Snow

Sung to: *London Bridge*

C
Winter fun is falling snow,

G₇   C
On my toes, on my nose.

Winter fun is falling snow,

G₇   C
I love winter.

Jean Warren

Fun for Everyone

Sung to: *Three Blind Mice*

C G₇ C   G₇ C
Winter fun, winter fun,

      G₇ C   G₇   C
Watch me slide, watch me run.

         G₇   C
The snow is falling all around,

C   G₇   C
It's covering up all of the ground,

         G₇   C
There's lots of fun for everyone,

       G₇ C
Winter fun.

Jean Warren

Little Groundhog

Little

Point index fingers of both hands away from body with palms facing each other and thumbs up (*l* handshapes). Move palms slightly toward each other.

Groundhog

Extend index fingers and thumbs of both hands (*g* handshapes) with palms facing each other. Place fingertips on cheeks and pull back twice to indicate whiskers.

Look All Around

Sung to: *I'm a Little Teapot*

C
See the **little groundhog,**
F   C
Furry and brown.
G₇   C
See the **little groundhog,**
G₇   C
Look all around.
                  F   C
If he sees his shadow, down he goes.
          F
There's more winter,
  G₇   C
Little groundhog knows.

Jean Warren

Little Groundhog

Sung to: *Little White Duck*

  C₇   F
There's a **little groundhog**

              C₇
Who lives down in the ground,

A **little groundhog**
             F
Who likes to look around.
    B♭   F
She comes outside on Groundhog's Day,
  G₇   C₇
If she sees her shadow then she runs away.
     F
There's a **little groundhog**

             C₇
Who loves to stay and play
             F
When spring's on its way.

Jean Warren

Can You Play?

Sung to: *Frere Jacques*

C
Little groundhog, little groundhog,

Can you play, can you play?

Popping up your head,

Popping up your head,

Can you play? Don't run away.

Little groundhog, little groundhog,

Can you play, can you play?

Running all around

On the cold hard ground

Can you play, please, please stay!

Little groundhog, little groundhog,

Can you play, can you play?

You can't see your shadow,

You can't see your shadow,

Here comes spring, hip hurray!

Jean Warren

I Love You

I Love You

Extend thumb, index and pinkie. This sign can remain stationary or move forward.

Yes, I Do

Sung to: *Three Blind Mice*

C G₇   C   G₇   C
I love you, I love you.

    G₇ C   G₇ C
Yes, I do, yes, I do.

        G₇   C
I love you every night and day,

        G₇   C
I love you when I work and play,

        G₇   C
I love you in so many ways.

   G₇   C
I love you.

Jean Warren

All the Time

Sung to: *Oh, My Darling Clementine*

   F
I love you, I love you,

         C₇
I love you all the time.

           F
And I hope, oh, yes, I hope

   C₇   F
You will be my valentine.

   F
I love you, I love you,

         C₇
I love you night and day.

           F
And I hope, oh, yes, I hope

   C₇   F
You will love me the same way.

Jean Warren

I Love You

Sung to: *Mary Had a Little Lamb*

C
Suzy, Suzy, **I love you.**

G₇   C
I love you, yes, I do.

C
Suzy, Suzy, **I love you,**

G₇   C
Yes, I do.

Substitute the names of your children for the names in the song.

Jean Warren

Write a Letter

Sung to: *A-Tisket, A-Tasket*

   C
I love you, I love you,

This is what I must do,

 G₇
Write a letter to you, love,

              C
And tell you that **I love you!**

   C
I love you, I love you,

This is what I hope you do,

 G₇
Write a letter back to me,

           C
And sign it **"I love you."**

Jean Warren

Hugs and Kisses

Hugs

Both fisted hands (*s* handshapes) move toward, and then touch, chest in a hug. Add *s* handshape for correct English grammar.

and

Right hand makes *5* handshape then moves to right and closes to *o* handshape.

Kisses

Fingertips touch lips, then cheek. Add *s* handshape for correct English grammar.

A Great Big Hug
Sung to: *The Wheels on the Bus*

        F
Oh, I just love your **hugs and kisses,**
C   **F**
Hugs and kisses, hugs and kisses.

Oh, I just love your **hugs and kisses,**
  C   **F**
Come, give me some.

       F
A great big hug and lots of kisses,
C   **F**
Lots of kisses, lots of kisses.

A great big hug and lots of kisses,
C   **F**
Ready? Here I come!

Jean Warren

Hugs and Kisses
Sung to: *My Bonnie Lies Over the Ocean*

    C   **F**   **C**
My mother says, "I love you."
         D₇   **G**
My father says, "I love you, too."
C   **F**   **C**
I give them **hugs and kisses,**
F   **G**   **C**
'Cause I love them, too!
      F
Hugs and kisses,
G   **C**
Hugs and kisses, I love you.
      F
Hugs and kisses,
G   **C**
Hugs and kisses for you.

Jean Warren

Everywhere
Sung to: *The Caissons Go Rolling Along*

  C
Hugs here, kisses there,

Hugs and kisses everywhere,
         G₇   **C**
When it's time to say goodbye.

Hugs here, kisses there,

Hugs and kisses everywhere,
         G₇   **C**
When it's time to say goodbye.

Oh, it's kiss, kiss, kiss,

Anyone we're going to miss?
        G₇   **C**
Hugs and kisses one last time.

Oh, we'll all sing this song,
        F   **C**
When we have to move along,
        G₇   **C**
Filled with **hugs and kisses,** goodbye.

Jean Warren

Be My Valentine

Be

Place hand with fingers together and thumb bent on palm (*b* handshape) at mouth. Move hand straight out.

My

Closed *5* handshape touches chest as if indicating possession.

Valentine

Third finger of each hand touches body over the heart, then third fingers draw an outline of a heart.

Valentine

Sung to: *Did You Ever See a Lassie?*

    F
Will you please **be my valentine,**
  C   F
My valentine, my valentine?

Will you please **be my valentine?**
C   F
For I love you.

    C₇ F
Here's hugs and kisses
    C₇ F
And lots of good wishes.

Will you please **be my valentine?**
C   F
For I love you.

Jean Warren

Here's My Card

Sung to: *Frere Jacques*

C
Be my valentine, be my valentine,

Here's my card, here's my card.

It says, "I love you,"

It says, "I love you."

Will you **be my valentine?**

Jean Warren

Please Be Mine

Sung to: *Pop Goes the Weasel*

D   A₇   D
Here's a special card for you,
     A₇   D
Will you please be mine?
       A₇   D
It's filled with hugs and lots of love,
A₇   D
Be my valentine!

Jean Warren

Be My Valentine

Sung to: *Row, Row, Row Your Boat*

C
Yes, yes, I love you,

Be my valentine.

Here's a heart just for you,
G   C
Won't you please be mine?

C
Yes, yes, watch me close,

Watch me while I sign.

I love you, yes, I do,
G   C
Be my valentine.

Jean Warren

Wearing Green

Wearing

Place thumbs of *5* handshapes on chest and move down and out. This is actually the sign for clothing.

Green

Extend index finger and thumb of right hand (*g* handshape) at a 45-degree angle from body with palm facing left. Shake hand.

Oh, Dear

Sung to: *Oh Dear, What Can the Matter Be?*

C
Oh dear, Ryan's not **wearing green,**

G₇
Oh dear, Meghan's not **wearing green,**

C
Oh dear, Jamie's not **wearing green,**

G₇   C
They need green bows right now.

(Hand out green bows.)

C
Yes, yes, now Ryan's **wearing green,**

G₇
Yes, yes, now Meghan's **wearing green,**

C
Yes, yes, now Jamie's **wearing green,**

G₇   C
Happy St. Patrick's Day!

Substitute the names of your children for the names in the song.

Jean Warren

On St. Patrick's Day

Sung to: *The Muffin Man*

G
Everyone is **wearing green,**

C   D
Wearing green, wearing green.

G
Everyone is **wearing green,**

D   G
On St. Patrick's Day.

Jean Warren

Oh, What Fun

Sung to: *Jingle Bells*

F
Wearing green, wearing green,

Wearing green today.

C₇   F
Oh, what fun it is to be

G₇   C₇
Wearing green today.

F
Green top hats, green striped shirts,

Oh, what fun today.

C₇   F
I just love **wearing green**

C₇   F
On St. Patrick's Day.

Jean Warren

Wearing Green

Sung to: *Three Blind Mice*

C   G₇   C   G₇   C
Wearing green, wearing green,

G₇   C   G₇   C
Prettiest sight I have seen.

G₇   C
Wearing green is so fun today,

C   G₇   C
Wearing green and dancing this way,

G₇   C
Wearing green on St. Patrick's Day,

G₇   C
Wearing green.

Jean Warren

Come Fly a Kite

Come

Index fingers of both hands, with palms facing self, alternately roll toward body.

Fly a Kite

Left index finger touches right palm. Move hands upward indicating a flying kite.

Come Fly a Kite

Sung to: *The Farmer in The Dell*

Oh, **come fly a kite,**

Oh, **come fly a kite,**

Heigh-ho, the derry-oh,
D   A₇   D
Oh, **come fly a kite.**

D
First we'll fly it high,

First we'll fly it high,

Heigh-ho, the derry-oh,
            A₇   D
Come fly a kite.

D
Then we'll fly it low,

Then we'll fly it low,

Heigh-ho, the derry-oh,
            A₇   D
Come fly a kite.

Jean Warren

Up in the Sky

Sung to: *On Top of Old Smoky*

C   F   C
Come fly a kite way up in the sky,
            G₇   C
Watch it climb up, up so high.
            F   C
Come fly a kite and watch it sail,
            G₇   C
Across the sky waving its tail.

Jean Warren

Oh, Let's Go Fly a Kite

Sung to: *Here We Go Looby Loo*

C
Will you **come fly a kite?**
                          G₇
Will you **come fly a kite?**
C
Will you **come fly a kite,**
G₇   C
To make such a beautiful sight?

C
First it'll soar up high

Until it reaches the sky.

And then it'll come down low
        G₇   C
And loop around just so.

C
Will you **come fly a kite?**
                          G₇
Will you **come fly a kite?**
C
Will you **come fly a kite,**
        G₇   C
To make such a beautiful sight?

Jean Warren

The Wind Is Blowing

The Wind Is Blowing

Place 5 handshapes in front of body with palms facing each other. Move hands back and forth to indicate the wind.

I See

Sung to: *Oh, What a Beautiful Morning*

C   B♭ F
I see **the wind is blowing,**
C   G₇
I see the trees bend low.
C   F F#dim
I see **the wind is blowing,**
C G₇   C
I see the clothes all blow.

Substitute the names of other things that
blow in the wind for *clothes.*

Jean Warren

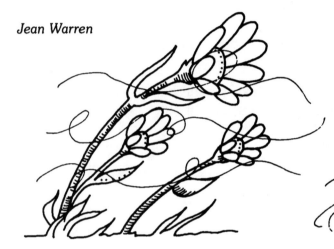

The Wind Is Blowing

Sung to: *Ten Little Indians*

C
One little, two little hats are blowing,
G₇
Three little, four little hats are blowing,
C
Five little, six little hats are blowing,
 G₇   C
See, **the wind is blowing.**

Substitute the names of other things that
blow in the wind for *hats.*

Jean Warren

Just Watch Them Blow

Sung to: *The Farmer in the Dell*

    D
The trees are bending low,

The hats fly to and fro.

Heigh-ho, just watch them blow,
 A₇   D
The wind is blowing so.

    D
The kites are in the sky,

The flags are flying high.

Heigh-ho, just watch them blow,
     A₇ D
The wind is blowing by.

Jean Warren

Blowing All Around

Sung to: *Found a Peanut*

      F
The wind is blowing,

The wind is blowing,
         C₇
The wind is blowing all around.
        F
All the hats and leaves and papers
 C₇   F
Are landing on the ground.

Jean Warren

Signing Is Fun

Signing

Index fingers of both hands, with palms facing each other, move in alternating circles toward body. An *i* handshape twists to right to add *-ing* for correct English grammar.

Is

Right pinkie (*i* handshape) starts on lower lip and moves straight out.

Fun

Index and middle fingers of right hand (*h* handshape) touch nose, then move to index and middle fingers of left hand. Both hands are palms down.

Learn to Sign

Sung to: *Did You Ever See a Lassie?*

F
Would you like to learn to sign,
C   F
To sign, to sign?

Would you like to learn to sign?
C   F
Signing is fun.
     C   F
Your fingers can talk,
     C   F
Like your feet can walk.

Would you like to learn to sign?
C   F
Signing is fun.

Jean Warren

Signing Is Fun

Sung to: *When Johnny Comes Marching Home*

     Em
Oh, **signing is fun** for everyone,
     G
Come sign today.
     Em
Oh, **signing is fun** for everyone,
     G   B₇
Hip, hip hurray!
     G   D₇
We'll sign a song, it won't take long,
     Fm   B₇
We'll raise our voices and sing along.
     Em Am   Em
Oh, we'll all sign a song
B₇   Em
'Cause **signing is fun.** Hurray!

Jean Warren

Let's Sign

Sung to: *Skip to My Lou*

D
Signing is fun, wouldn't you say?
A₇
Signing is fun, let's sign today.
D
Signing is fun, we'll sign this way.
A₇   D
Signing is fun, my darling.

Jean Warren

While We Work and Play

Sung to: *Row, Row, Row Your Boat*

C
Let's sign, sign, everyday

While we work and play.

Signing is fun for everyone,
     G   C
Let's sing and sign today.

Jean Warren

Spring Is Here

Spring

Fingers on right hand move up twice through left hand to indicate plants and flowers growing from the ground.

Is

Right pinkie (*i* handshape) starts on lower lip and moves straight out.

Here

Both hands, with palms up, move out in opposite circles.

What a Sight
Sung to: *Skip to My Lou*

F
Spring is here, snow's gone away,
C₇
Spring is here, what do you say?
F
Spring is here, let's dance all day,
C₇   F
Spring is here, my darling.

F
Spring is here, there is more light,
C₇
Spring is here, with flowers bright.
F
Spring is here, oh, what a sight,
C₇   F
Spring is here, my darling.

Jean Warren

Spring Is Here
Sung to: *London Bridge*

C
Leaves are growing on the trees,
G₇   C
On the trees, on the trees.

Leaves are growing on the trees,
G₇   C
Spring is here.

Additional verses: All the grass is turning
green; See the young birds in their nests;
Watch the flowers start to grow.

*Frank Dally
Ankeny, IA*

Give a Cheer
Sung to: *Frere Jacques*

C
Spring is here, spring is here,

Give a cheer, give a cheer.

No more storms that blow,

No more ice and snow.

Give a cheer, **spring is here.**

Jean Warren

Spring Every Day
Sung to: *Jingle Bells*

C
Spring is here,

Spring is here,

Spring is here today.
F   C
I just wish that it was spring,
G   C
Each and every day.

C
Spring is here,

Spring is here,

Spring is here today.
F   C
Crocuses and robins,
G   C
All are on their way.

Jean Warren

Rain Is Falling

Rain Is Falling

Bend fingers of both hands with palms facing down. Move hands down sharply twice to indicate rain.

Pitter, Patter

Sung to: *Frere Jacques*

C
Rain is falling, rain is falling

On the ground, what a sound.

Pitter, pitter, patter,

Pitter, pitter, patter,

Rain is falling, rain is falling.

Jean Warren

Zim-Bam, Zim-Bam

Sung to: *Twinkle, Twinkle, Little Star*

C   F   C
Zim-bam, zim-bam, zim-bam-bee,
G₇   C   G₇   C
Rain is falling on the tree.
        G₇   C   G₇
Zim-bam, zim-bam, zim-bam-by,
C   G₇   C   G₇
Rain is falling from the sky.
C   F   C
Zim-bam, zim-bam, zim-bam-boo,
G₇   C   G₇   C
Rain is falling on us too.

Jean Warren

Rain Is Falling in the Zoo

Sung to: *Found a Peanut*

F
Rain is falling, rain is falling,
           C₇
Rain is falling in the zoo.
               F
And the animals are dancing,
       C₇   F
'Cause it feels so good to do.

F
See the bears, see the elephants,
             C₇
See the jumping kangaroo.
            F
We are dancing in the rain,
   C₇   F
Rain is falling on me too!

Jean Warren

Rain Is Falling on You

Sung to: *Happy Birthday*

          F   C
Rain is falling on you,
              F
Rain is falling on me,
                B♭
Rain is falling on everyone,
         F   C   F
Rain is falling, yippee!

Jean Warren

My Easter Basket

My

Closed *5* handshape touches chest as if indicating possession.

Easter

Fingers on both hands "sit" on bent thumbs (*e* handshapes). Hands circle in opposite directions.

Basket

Right *b* handshape (four fingers together with thumb bent on palm) touches left wrist, then flips and touches lower forearm.

Pick Up Eggs

Sung to: *The Paw Paw Patch*

F
Pick up the eggs and put 'em in

My Easter basket,

C₇
Pick up the eggs and put 'em in

My Easter basket,

F
Pick up the eggs and put 'em in

My Easter basket,

C₇   F
Early on Easter morning.

Jean Warren

Where Is My Easter Basket?

Sung to: *Skip to My Lou*

F
Where's **my Easter basket?** I don't know.

C₇
Where's **my Easter basket?** I don't know.

F
Where's **my Easter basket?** I don't know.

C₇   F
I have hunted high and low.

Jean Warren

The Easter Bunny

Sung to: *Old MacDonald Had a Farm*

           C   F   C
The Easter Bunny came to town,

           G₇   C
With **my Easter basket.**

                          F   C
He went hopping all around,

           G₇   C
With **my Easter basket.**

                    C
With a hop-hop here,

And a hop-hop there,

Here a hop, there a hop,

Everywhere a hop-hop.

                          F   C
The Easter Bunny came to town,

           G₇   C
With **my Easter basket.**

Jean Warren

My Easter Basket

Sung to: *I'm a Little Teapot*

C
Here's **my Easter basket**

F   C
Full of treats,

G₇   C   G₇   C
Colorful eggs and lots of sweets.

                    F   C
I get all excited when they say,

                    F   G₇   C
"The Easter Bunny is on his way."

Jean Warren

Funny Little Bunny

Funny

Place the index and middle fingers (*h* handshape), with palm facing self, on nose and pull down. Repeat motion.

Little

Point index fingers of both hands away from self with palms facing each other and thumbs up (*l* handshapes). Move palms slightly toward each other.

Bunny

Right *b* handshape, with palm facing left, sits on wrist of left *b* handshape, with palm facing right. Bend fingers at knuckles twice to indicate the movement of a bunny's ears.

Down the Lane
Sung to: *Mary Had a Little Lamb*

C
Once I met a **funny little bunny,**
G₇   C
Funny little bunny, funny little bunny.

Once I met a **funny little bunny**
G₇   C
Hopping down the lane.

Jean Warren

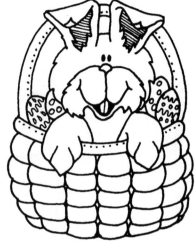

Funny Little Bunny
Sung to: *The Bear Went Over the Mountain*

          C   F   C
The **funny little bunny,**
G₇   C
The **funny little bunny,**
                        F
The **funny little bunny**
G₇   C
Hopped right into town.

(Hop.)

Substitute other action words for *hop.* Have your children act out the motion named.

Jean Warren

Carrot Patch
Sung to: *Yankee Doodle*

    C   G
A **funny little bunny**
C   G
Went to town one day.
C   F
He was looking for some food
G₇   C
And a place to stay.
F
Funny little bunny,
C
Did you find a home?
F
Yes, I found a carrot patch,
      C   G₇   C
Now I won't have to roam.

Jean Warren

Hop, Hop, Hop
Sung to: *The Wheels on the Bus*

              F
Oh, the **funny little bunny**

Went hop, hop, hop,
C
Hop, hop, hop,
F
Hop, hop, hop.

Oh, the **funny little bunny**

Went hop, hop, hop,
C   F
All over town.

Jean Warren

May Basket

May

Fingers on right hand move up twice through left hand to indicate plants and flowers growing from the ground. This sign is also used for "spring."

Basket

Right *b* handshape (four fingers together with thumb bent on palm) touches left wrist, then flips and touches lower forearm.

A Basket, a Basket
Sung to: *A-Tisket, A-Tasket*

C
A basket, a basket,

A beautiful **May basket.**

G7
I made a basket for my mom,

C
But on the way I lost it.

C
I lost it, I lost it,

My beautiful **May basket.**

G7
Maybe if I go and search,

C
Somewhere I will find it.

C
I found it, I found it,

My beautiful **May basket.**

G7
I'll fill it up with flowers bright,

C
I know my mom will love it.

C
She'll love it, she'll love it,

My beautiful **May basket.**

G7
I made a basket for my mom,

C
A beautiful **May basket.**

Jean Warren

May Basket
Sung to: *Did You Ever See a Lassie?*

F
Did you ever see a **May basket,**

C7   F
A **May basket,** a **May basket?**

Did you ever see a **May basket**

C7   F
That looked so good?

C7   F
I worked for hours,

C7   F
Then filled it with flowers.

F
Did you ever see a **May basket**

C7   F
That looked so good?

Jean Warren

Made By Me
Sung to: *I'm a Little Teapot*

C
Here's a little **May basket**

F   C
Made by me,

G7   C
Filled with flowers,

G7   C
Pretty as can be.

I'll hang this **May basket**

F   C
On a door today,

F   G7   C
Then take off and run away.

Elizabeth McKinnon

Flowers Are Blooming

Flowers

Fingertips of right hand rest on thumb (o hand-shape). Place hand under left nostril and move to right nostril as if smelling a picked flower. Add s handshape for correct English grammar.

Are

Crossed fingers (r handshape) of right hand, with palm facing left, start on lower lip and move straight out.

Blooming

Both hands make o handshapes, with finger-tips touching, and open to 5 handshapes, with palms touching, to indicate the opening of a flower's petals. An i handshape twists to right to add -ing for correct English grammar.

It Must Be Spring

Sung to: *When Johnny Comes Marching Home*

Em
The **flowers are blooming,** it must be spring,

G
Hurray, hurray!

Em
The **flowers are blooming,** let's all sing,

B₇
Hurray, hurray!

G   D₇
I see crocuses on the hills,

Em   B₇
Flowering trees and daffodils.

        Em Am Em
Oh, it's all so gay,

B₇   Em
The **flowers are blooming** today.

Jean Warren

In the Month of May

Sung to: *Jingle Bells*

F
Climbing bells, daffodils,

Flowers are blooming today.

C₇   F
What a lovely time of year

G₇   C₇
Is the month of May.

F
Budding trees, happy bees,

Flowers are blooming today.

C₇   F
What a lovely time of year

C₇   F
Is the month of May.

Jean Warren

The World Is Filled With Color

Sung to: *Go In and Out the Window*

F   C
The **flowers are blooming** brightly,

                                     F
The **flowers are blooming** brightly,

                                     C
The **flowers are blooming** brightly,

                          F
The world is filled with color.

Jean Warren

The Flowers Are Blooming

Sung to: *London Bridge*

C
The **flowers are blooming** everywhere,

G₇   C
Everywhere, everywhere.

The **flowers are blooming** everywhere,

G₇   C
What a lovely day.

C
The **flowers are blooming** everywhere,

G₇   C
Everywhere, everywhere.

The **flowers are blooming** everywhere,

G₇   C
In the month of May.

Jean Warren

In My Garden

In

Flat *o* handshape of right hand goes into *c* handshape of left hand.

My

Closed *5* handshape touches chest as if indicating possession.

Garden

With right hand in front of left, form *g* handshapes with right fingers facing left and left fingers facing right. Move both handshapes so that fingers face out to form a square.

Out in My Garden

Sung to: *Down by the Station*

F
Out **in my garden**
C   F
Early in the morning,

See the little vegetables
C   F
All in a row.

See the rows of carrots
C   F
And the rows of peas.

Water, hoe, grow, grow,
C   F
In my garden, please.

Jean Warren

Dig and Hoe

Sung to: *My Bonnie Lies Over
the Ocean*

       C   F   C
In my garden I like to work,

              D$_7$
In my garden I dig in the ground.
       C   F   C
In my garden I grow great big vegetables
   F   G   C
And have lots of flowers around.

       F
Dig, hoe, dig, hoe,
G   C
In my garden things grow, grow, grow.
       F
Dig, hoe, dig, hoe,
G   C
In my garden things grow.

Jean Warren

Flower Garden

Sung to: *Mary Had a Little Lamb*

C
I will plant some flower seeds,
G$_7$ C
Flower seeds, flower seeds.

I will plant some flower seeds
G$_7$ C
In my garden.

C
I will water my flower seeds,
G$_7$ C
Flower seeds, flower seeds.

I will water my flower seeds
G$_7$ C
In my garden.

C
I will watch my flowers grow,
G$_7$ C
Flowers grow, flowers grow.

I will watch my flowers grow
G$_7$ C
In my garden.

C
I will pick some flowers today,
G$_7$ C
Flowers today, flowers today.

I will pick some flowers today
G$_7$ C
In my garden.

Jean Warren

Happy Mother's (Father's) Day

Happy

Tap chest with right palm, moving palm up and forward twice.

Mother's

Make a 5 handshape with right hand and rest thumb on chin. Wiggle fingers. Fisted right hand (s handshape) flips to left to show possession.

(Father's)

Make a 5 handshape with right hand and rest thumb on forehead. Wiggle fingers. Fisted right hand (s handshape) flips to left to show possession.

Day

Right hand, with index finger extended, moves to left across self to indicate the daily movement of the sun from east to west.

Happy Day

Sung to: *Happy Birthday*

Happy (Mother's/Father's) Day to you,
  F   F   C

Happy (Mother's/Father's) Day to you.
                         F

Happy (Mother's/Father's) Day dear

 B♭   B♭
(Mommy/Daddy),
    F   F   C F
Happy (Mother's/Father's) Day to you.

Jean Warren

May All Your Dreams Come True

Sung to: *Found a Peanut*

      F   F
Happy (Mother's/Father's) Day,

Happy (Mother's/Father's) Day,

                            C₇
Happy (Mother's/Father's) Day to you.

Happy (Mother's/Father's) Day,

      F   F
Happy (Mother's/Father's) Day,

  C₇   F
And may all your dreams come true.

Jean Warren

Very Much

Sung to: *Goodnight Ladies*

F
Happy, (Mother's/Father's) Day,

                      C
Happy (Mother's/Father's) Day,
F   B♭
Happy (Mother's/Father's) Day,
  F   C   F
I love you very much.

Kathleen Cubley

We Honor Them Today

Sung to: *The Battle Hymn of the Republic*

      C
I'd like to wish a **Happy (Mother's/**

Father's) Day to everyone.
F   F
(Mothers/Fathers) are so special

           C
To their daughters and their sons.

You work so hard, you never stop,

You take good care of us,
           G₇   C
And we honor you today.

Refrain:
C
Happy, **Happy (Mother's/Father's) Day,**
F   C
Happy, **Happy (Mother's/Father's) Day,**

Happy, **Happy (Mother's/Father's) Day,**
  G₇   C
And we honor you today.

Jean Warren

In the Summertime

In

Flat *o* handshape of right hand goes into *c* handshape of left hand.

the

Place thumb between first two fingers of right hand (*t* handshape). Move hand to right.

Summer

Wipe crooked index finger of right hand across forehead as if wiping away perspiration.

Time

Bent index finger of right hand taps wrist of left hand, where a watch is generally worn.

What Can I Do?

Sung to: *Oh, Dear, What Can the Matter Be?*

C
What can I do **in the summertime?**
G₇
What can I do **in the summertime?**
C
What can I do **in the summertime?**
G₇   C
I think I'll learn to swing.

Substitute other action phrases for *learn to swing.*

Jean Warren

In the Summertime

Sung to: *Frere Jacques*

C
I love swimming, I love swimming,

Yes, I do, yes, I do,

In the summertime,

In the summertime.

How about you? How about you?

Substitute the names of other activities for *swimming.*

Jean Warren

Let's Go

Sung to: *Row, Row, Row Your Boat*

C
Let's go to a camp

In the summertime.

We will learn to swim and sail
G   C
In the summertime.

C
Let's go to the zoo

In the summertime.

We will see the lions and bears
G   C
In the summertime.

C
Let's go to the farm

In the summertime.

We will feed the pigs and chicks
G   C
In the summertime.

Let your children make up additional verses as desired.

Jean Warren

Off We Go

Off We Go

Place closed 5 handshapes of both hands, with palms facing each other, in front of body. Right hand moves up, hits left hand and continues upward.

Off We Go

Sung to: *Mary Had a Little Lamb*

C
Buckle up, then **off we go,**
G₇   C
Off we go, off we go.

Buckle up, then **off we go,**
G₇   C
To our school.

Substitute other destinations for *school.*

Jean Warren

Traveling Song

Sung to: *If You're Happy and You Know It*

F   C
When we're all in the car, **off we go.**
                                     F
When we're all in the car, **off we go.**
              B♭
When we're all in the car,
       F
Then we can travel far.
              C   F
When we're all in the car, **off we go.**

F   C
When we're all in the bus, **off we go.**
                                     F
When we're all in the bus, **off we go.**
              B♭
When we're all in the bus,
       F
Then no one has to fuss.
              C   F
When we're all in the bus, **off we go.**

Jean Warren

When Everyone Is Ready

Sung to: *When Johnny Comes Marching Home*

        Em   G
When everyone is ready, then **off we go,**
        Em   G   B₇
When everyone is ready, then **off we go.**
        G   D₇
Let's form a line very straight,
Em   B₇
Then get started, I can't wait!.
                  Em Am Em B₇ Em
Oh, we're almost ready, then **off we go.**

Jean Warren

The People on the Bus

Sung to: *The Wheels on the Bus*

              F
Oh, the people on the bus say,
C   F
"Off we go, off we go, off we go."

Oh, the people on the bus say, **"Off we go,"**
C   F
All over town.

Jean Warren

The Sun Is Shining

The Sun

Right index finger draws a circle in the air to indicate the sun.

Is Shining

Right hand forms *o* handshape and drops down, opening to a *5* handshape to indicate light.

The Sun Is Shining

Sung to: *You Are My Sunshine*

The sun is shining,
[C]

The sun is shining,

The sun is shining out today.
[F] *[C]*

I want to hurry and get my work done,
[F] *[C]*

So I can go out and play.
[G₇] *[C]*

Jean Warren

Look, the Sun Is Shining Bright

Sung to: *Twinkle, Twinkle, Little Star*

The sun is shining, shining bright,
[C] *[F]* *[C]*

The sun is shining, bringing light.
[G₇] *[C]* *[G₇]* *[C]*

The sun is shining, a wonderous thing,
[G₇] *[C]* *[G₇]*

When I see it, I just sing.
[C] *[G₇]* *[C]* *[G₇]*

The sun is shining, shining bright,
[C] *[F]* *[C]*

The sun is shining, bringing light.
[G₇] *[C]* *[G₇]* *[C]*

Jean Warren

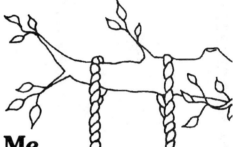

Sing a Song of Summer

Sung to: *Sing a Song of Sixpence*

See the sun is shining,
[C]

The sun is shining bright.
[G₇]

See the sun is shining,

The days are filled with light.
[C]

Be happy every moment,

No matter what you do.
[G₇]

When the sun is shining

Just let the sunshine through.
[C]

Jean Warren

Sun on Me

Sung to: *Frere Jacques*

The sun is shining,
[C]

The sun is shining,

All around,

On the ground.

The sun is on the tree,

The sun is on me,

Shadows found,

All around.

Jean Warren

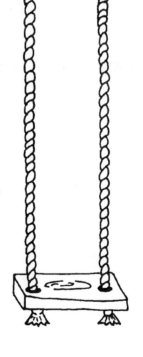

Along the Trail

Along the Trail

Closed 5 handshapes of both hands, with palms facing each other, move forward and parallel to each other in a winding motion to indicate a path.

Over the River

Sung to: *Over the River*

C
Over the river, **along the trail,**
    F   C
The hikers march along.
   Dm   C   Am
And as they go, they love to sing
    D₇   G
Their favorite hiking song.

C
Over the river, **along the trail,**
    F   C
They love to hike and sing.
   Dm   C   Am
They're filled with all the wonders
   G   C
A nature hike can bring.

Jean Warren

Along the Trail

Sung to: *Frere Jacques*

C
Let's go marching, let's go marching,

Along the trail, along the trail.

I love to march fast,

I love to march slow,

Along the trail, along the trail.

Substitute the names of other actions
for *marching*.

Jean Warren

March and Sing

Sung to: *The Mulberry Bush*

D
Along the trail we march and sing,
A₇
March and sing, march and sing.
D
Along the trail we march and sing,
A₇   D
Along the trail today.

Additional verses: Along the trail we huff and
puff; skip and whistle; swing our arms.

Jean Warren

I Met a Bear

Sung to: *Skip to My Lou*

F
I met a bear **along the trail,**
G₇
I met a bear **along the trail,**
F
I met a bear **along the trail,**
  C₇   F
I better step aside.

Additional verses: I met a skunk;
squirrel; deer.

Jean Warren

Red, White and Blue

Red

Pull index finger down from lips to indicate lip color or lipstick.

White

Five handshape touches chest, then moves away from self into o handshape.

and

Right hand makes 5 handshape, then moves to right and closes to o handshape.

Blue

Form b handshape (four fingers together with thumb bent on palm) with right hand, palm facing left. Shake hand.

Over Fields of Grain

Sung to: *The Caissons Go Rolling Along*

C
Over fields of grain,

And every mountain range

      G₇
Flies the flag of **red, white and blue.**   C

It's our flag and we know

That wherever we shall go

       G₇
There's our flag of **red, white and blue.** C

It's for you and me,

    F   C
And all that we can see.

                      G₇
It's our flag of **red, white and blue.**

  C   E₇
It's our flag you see.

  F   C
And it's for you and me.

     G₇   C
It's the flag of **red, white and blue.**

Jean Warren

The Red, White and Blue

Sung to: *When the Saints Come Marching In*

           C
Oh, when the flag comes marching in,

                        G₇
Oh, when the flag comes marching in.

  C   F
How I love to see its three colors,

  C   G₇ C
The **red, white and blue.**

Jean Warren

Down at the Flagpole

Sung to: *Down by the Station*

C
Down at the flagpole,

G   C
Early in the morning,

We will raise our flag,

    G   C
The **red, white and blue.**

C
We stand at attention,

    G   C
It's something that we do.

We salute the colors,

    G   C
The **red, white and blue.**

Jean Warren

A Flag for Me and You

Sung to: *Three Blind Mice*

C   G₇   C
Red, white and blue,

       G₇   C
Red, white and blue,

    G₇ C
A flag for me,

    G₇ C
A flag for you.

        G₇   C
It is the flag of our great nation,

        G₇   C
It's honored by each generation.

       G₇   C
Join me now in a celebration,

    G₇   C
Red, white and blue.

Jean Warren

Happy Birthday

Happy

Tap chest with right palm, moving palm up and forward twice.

Birthday

Closed 5 handshape of right hand touches upper abdomen, then moves into the up-turned palm of left hand to indicate arrival.

We All Wish You Well

Sung to: *The Farmer in the Dell*

D
We all wish you well,

We think you are swell.

Happy birthday, Katie,
A₇   D
We all wish you well.

D
We've come to celebrate,

We think you are great.

Happy birthday, Katie,
A₇   D
We've come to celebrate.

Substitute the name of your birthday
child for *Katie.*

Jean Warren

Come, Let's Sing

Sung to: *The Bear Went Over
the Mountain*

C   F   C
Come, let's sing **"happy birthday,"**
G₇   C
Come, let's sing **"happy birthday,"**
C   F
Come, let's sing **"happy birthday,"**
C   G₇
To Johnny on his day.

Substitute the name of your birthday child
for the name *Johnny.*

Jean Warren

Happy Birthday

Sung to: *Found a Peanut*

F
Happy birthday,

Happy birthday,
C₇
It is Andrew's birthday.

F
We wish you joy and laughter
C₇   F
And lots of fun today.

Substitute the name of your birthday
child for *Andrew.*

Jean Warren

If You're Older

Sung to: *If You're Happy and You Know It*

F   C₇
If you're older on this day, stand up now.

F
If you're older on this day, stand up now.

B♭
If you're older on this day,

F
Then we all want to say,

C   F
"Happy, happy, **happy birthday!"**

Repeat several times, substituting other actions
for *stand up now.*

Jean Warren

Song Index

Sign Phrase Index

Sign Language Alphabet

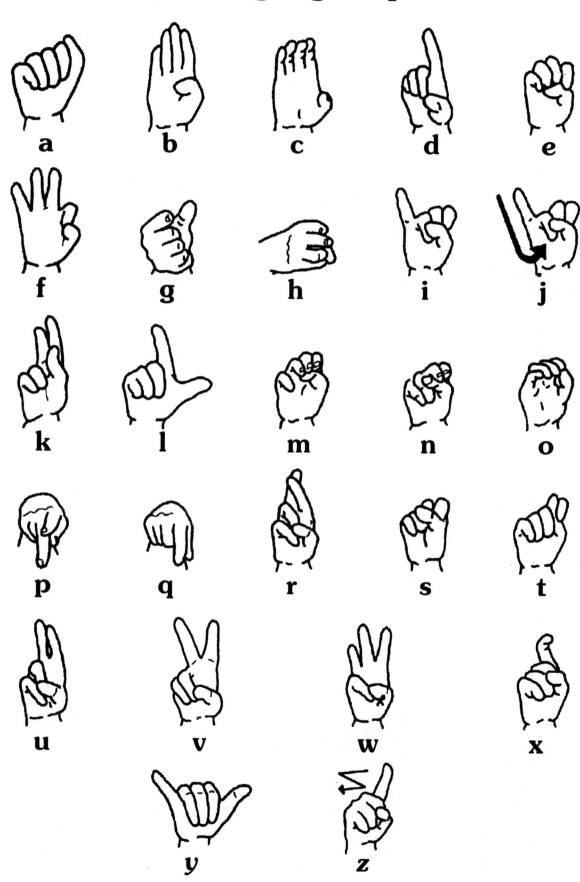

This page reprinted with permission from Sugar Sign Press.

NEW! Early Learning Resources

For Teachers

Art Series

Great ideas for exploring art with children ages 3 to 6! Easy, inexpensive activities encourage enjoyable art experiences in a variety of ways.

Cooperative Art • Outdoor Art • Special Day Art

The Best of Totline—Bear Hugs

This new resource is a collection of some of Totline's best ideas for fostering positive behavior.

Celebrating Childhood Posters

Inspire parents, staff, and yourself with these endearing posters with poems by Jean Warren.

The Children's Song
Patterns
Pretending
Snowflake Splendor
The Heart of a Child
Live Like the Child
The Light of Childhood
A Balloon
The Gift of Rhyme

Circle Time Series

Teachers will discover quick, easy ideas to incorporate into their lessons when they gather children together for this important time of the day.

Introducing Concepts at Circle Time
Music and Dramatics at Circle Time
Storytime Ideas for Circle Time

Empowering Kids

This unique series tackles behavioral issues in typical Totline fashion—practical ideas for empowering young children with self-esteem and basic social skills.

Problem-Solving Kids
Can-Do Kids

Theme-A-Saurus

Two new theme books join this popular Totline series!

Transportation Theme-A-Saurus
Field Trip Theme-A-Saurus

For Parents

My First Coloring Book Series

These coloring books are truly appropriate for toddlers—black backgrounds with white illustrations. That means no lines to cross and no-lose coloring fun! Bonus stickers included!

All About Colors
All About Numbers
Under the Sea
Over and Under
Party Animals
Tops and Bottoms

Happy Days

Seasonal fun with rhymes and songs, snack recipes, games, and arts and crafts.

Pumpkin Days • Turkey Days • Holly Days • Snowy Days

Little Builder Stacking Cards

Each game box includes 48 unique cards with different scenes printed on each side. Children can combine the cards that bend in the middle with the flat cards to form simple buildings or tall towers!

Castle
The Three Little Pigs

Rainy Day Fun

Turn rainy-day blahs into creative, learning fun! These creative Totline ideas turn a home into a jungle, post office, grocery store, and more!

Rhyme & Reason Sticker Workbooks

These age-appropriate workbooks combine language and thinking skills for a guaranteed fun learning experience. More than 100 stickers!

Up in Space • All About Weather • At the Zoo • On the Farm • Things That Go • Under the Sea

Theme Calendars

Weekly activity ideas in a nondated calendar for exploring the seasons with young children.

Toddler Theme Calendar
Preschool Theme Calendar
Kindergarten Theme Calendar

Totline® PUBLICATIONS

**Start right,
start bright!**